I0014540

AFFILIATE MARKETING SECRETS

Taking your internet business to the next level.

IQ PRESS, INC.

Disclaimer

CONTENTS

ACKNOWLEDGMENTS

IQ Press, Inc. is a small publishing company dedicated to providing access to educational materials primarily in small business start-up and development. Their mission is to bring the reader useful information that can be implemented with a small capital outlay and generate income streams for the reader to implement.

We hope you enjoy these reports and that they will help improve your life.

www.IQPress.org

i

Chapter 1: Affiliate Marketing - Definition and Overview

Affiliate marketing is a way of making money online. It's really a simple concept. When you are an affiliate marketer, you promote a product, service, or site for a business, and you as a publisher get rewarded for doing so.

In most cases, you find products related to your niche and offer them on your website or blog. You promote the products and post a link on your site where they can purchase the products. Then, when someone follows th22at link to buy something, you earn a commission. The commissions can be either a percentage of the sale or a fixed amount. You've seen links to other sites when you've read other people's blogs. These links make the blogger money.

For example: I write a book about affiliate marketing. Your blog is focused on tips to make money online. You actually promote and sell the book from your site. You get a percentage of the sale. It's like being paid an advertising or marketing fee.

You may also sell other products that are related to your site. For example: You blog about cooking and recipes. There are endless numbers of cooking related appliances or utensils you could sell from your site to make it easier for them to prepare those recipes.

In other cases, you might earn an amount when someone follows the link and take some kind of action such as: sign up for something with their email address or complete a survey with their name and address.

Your earnings are usually tracked by using a link that has a code embedded in it. This link is only used by you. They may also be tracked when the advertiser gives you a coupon code. You've probably followed a link from another site at one time or another online. You've also probably bought something where you enter a code. When customers do this, you make money without doing a thing. They do the work for you.

There are a few factors that help make your affiliate marketing successful.

These include:

•   The amount of traffic you have. The higher the traffic, the greater your earning potential will be.

- The quality of the products you recommend. Recommending junk products can really hurt you, so you want to make sure what you recommend will be a real value to your readers.

- The amount of trust your readers have in you. If you have established trust, your readers are more likely to click on the link.

Publishers like affiliate marketing for the obvious reason...you get paid while someone else does the work. You may be in bed asleep and still be earning money. If you find a product that is relevant to your niche, your earnings can be pretty good if you have a large following.

You may be wondering why an affiliate seller would pay people for advertising in this manner. It's a matter of cost. They may pay a lot of money for an advertising campaign that doesn't pay off. With affiliate marketing, however, they only pay when the advertising pays off. If they have a good network of affiliates they may make less per sale, but overall, their sales will increase.

If you have a good level of trust with the people who read your blog, they will trust that you wouldn't recommend something they wouldn't like. This will cause them to at least look at what you're recommending. With the right sales pitch online, you can make it something they "must" have. If they purchase something from you and it is a good product that they like, they're more apt to buy another. They'll also pass on where they got it. That will lead more traffic to your site and increase your sales.

Chapter 2: Advantages and Benefits of Affiliate Marketing

If you're looking for a way to make money online, you should consider affiliate marketing. There are numerous benefits to becoming an affiliate. These include:

• There's no production cost - If you wanted to set up a business selling products online, you'd have to buy, ship, and store the products. It can be costly. If you have an affiliate program, production cost isn't an issue. The merchant has already paid for the development of the product.

• The set-up cost is low - You probably already have a desk, an internet connection, and a computer. That's all you need to get started.

• There are no fees or licenses to pay—Affiliate programs are usually free to join. Your geographic market reach is as big as your ability to promote your site. The internet is a worldwide marketplace. You can take advantage of this market.

- You can sell almost anything - There are few blog sites that wouldn't be able to find a product to promote that is related to their niche, but they are limited. Almost everything you can think of is sold online. There are thousands of affiliate programs, so it is easy to find products related to your current site or the site you are planning to set up.

- You don't have to handle any sales to make money from them - You have no inventory, no order processing, and no shipping to deal with. You make money from sales by promoting the products, not having to take care of the actual sales process.

- You can work from home - If you've ever had a long commute to work, you can really appreciate the ability to work from home. It's also a great way to get to spend more time with your family. You won't have the normal work expenses like gas, buying lunch, wardrobe, etc. You can work in the comfort of your own home – even in your pajamas if you want.

- If you have your computer with you, you can work from anywhere in the world - Have you ever wanted to travel, but taking off from work isn't an option? If so, affiliate marketing is perfect. You take your office with you. You wouldn't have to spend more than a few hours a day working, and you could visit anywhere you wanted and still be able to work, as long as you have an internet connection.

• There is a minimal level of risk - If you try to sell a product and it isn't making you enough money, you just stop selling it and try something else. All you have to do is take down your links and promote another product. It's that simple. You don't have to worry about being stuck with inventory or in a long-term contract that binds you to promote a product that doesn't sell.

• There is potential for high income - With your own online affiliate business, your potential for income is only limited by your efforts. Granted, not everyone makes a lot of money. You have to be willing to put forth the effort to find, set up, and promote the products. If you promote your products well and build traffic to your site, you can have a successful affiliate business.

Chapter 3: How Does Affiliate Marketing Work?

People who want to make money online usually struggle with creating a website, ads, sales and closing scripts. They also have their own merchant account services. A few people may actually enjoy going through that process, but for those who don't have the time, energy, or desire to put forth that much energy, affiliate marketing is ideal.

If you want to make money online using affiliate marketing, you don't have to worry about the setup. Most companies will provide you with information about the product and product reviews or testimonials that you can use. However, many people prefer to write their own personal product reviews.

Your payment gateway is set up by the business. You don't have to worry about handling the money or dealing with refunds.

Here are a few different areas of affiliate marketing and how it works in these areas:

1. What You Offer

All you need to do is use a search engine like Google, and you can find a list of affiliate programs. A broad search will let you

discover every program out there. You may want to only be an affiliate for products in your niche. If so, then just search for the niche you're interested in such as:

- Electronics Affiliate Programs

- Cosmetic Affiliate Programs

- Food Preparation Affiliate Programs

Whatever niche you want can probably be found with a simple online search for it. You may want to look at some of the affiliate resources that are popular like Clickbank.com or Amazon.com. There will be a distributor form. It has the terms and conditions that tell you how you're allowed to sell their products and what the commission is.

Here are a few good tips to remember when you're selecting a product:

1. First, you need to have either a website or blog to make decent earnings. If you don't at least have a blog, you should begin one today. Focus it on topics that you are interested in and know a lot about. With each Clickbank product there are some statistics mentioned, let me explain them:

2.   Select products that are related to the niche of your website/blog.

3.   Find items where you'll end up making at least $20 per sale.

4.   A good gravity range for selecting products is a range of 50-120.

5.   There are some products out there that offer up to 75% commission. It is good to select those where you'll make at least 50% or more expensive products with a good commission.

6.   Find products with good landing pages. If you're not satisfied with the way the website looks for the product you're promoting, it will probably be hard for you to convince your audience to buy those products. Look for well-written sales copy and strong guarantees.

7.   The best way to sell the products you promote is to find those products that help your readers solve a problem.

2. Cost

It is usually free to sign up to be an affiliate. Some programs require a small monthly or annual fee. This helps the business pay for their website, training, overhead, and use of their payment processors.

Some vendors will require that the affiliate purchase the product in order to make the biggest commission. They feel you should have the product and use it so you'll be prepared to give it a better recommendation based on your first-hand experience working with the product.

3.   Earning commissions

The percentage of commission will vary depending on the vendor's terms and conditions. There isn't a set commission, and the amount of commission can vary greatly.

The commission you receive is based on these things:

•   Commission structure of the product you wish to sell

•   The number of people who purchase the product—this will depend on how you advertise it and how well you connect with the audience you are targeting

•   Whether or not the affiliate program is a program that is leveraged

It is practically impossible to truly determine how much you will make. The variables are just too great. It really depends on you.

4. Receiving commissions

Every vendor has their own method of paying commissions. There are vendors that will pay you on a regular basis no matter how little or how much you earn. Others, however, will not pay you until you reach a minimum threshold. They can pay you in different intervals such as: Instantly, weekly, bi-monthly, monthly, or quarterly.

The types of payment you receive can vary as well. You can be paid by using ways such as: A check in the mail, PayPal, direct deposit, Federal Express, or pay through a debit card.

5. Tracking sales

You will be assigned your own ID. It will be built into your website URL when you sign up and are approved to be an affiliate.

It works like this. Let's say you find a company named www.letsgodecocrazy.com. You find the site and sign as an affiliate for their product. They will ask you for a user name. You select "zigzag." The username can be built into your URL as a way to advertise. It may be www.letsgodecocrazy.com/zigzag or http://zigzag.letsgodecocrazy.com.

Sometimes the company assigns you something different. Sometimes it just looks like a very long line of numbers, letters, and characters. Whatever is used, that's the URL you need to use to send your traffic to. When they buy by clicking on your link, you get the agreed upon commission.

6. Sign up process

Research and find an affiliate that right for you. When you find it, go to their website. Look for something like, "Affiliates," "Join Affiliate Program," or "Partners Program." Carefully read their terms and conditions. View all the products they offer. You want to make sure they are what you're looking for.

If you clearly understand what you can and can't do when selling the product and you feel the commission rate is sufficient, sign up. They should direct you to a form to fill out online. If you don't find an affiliate application, you can either call them or email them and request one.

They will want to know your name, address, phone, email, and if they give you a choice, how you want to be paid. Be prepared to give them your Social Security number. This is for tax purposes, and you will receive a 1099 at the end of the year. Some request it at the time of the application and others hold your earnings until they receive it. If you don't provide it within the time frame requested, however, you will forfeit any earnings you've made.

7. Marketing

There are many different ways you can market your product/service online. Sometimes, it will depend on what the product or service is. It will also depend on you and where your talents and preferences lie. Here are a few of them:

•   Blogging - If you like to write, you may want to write a blog post that describes the benefits of your product/service. You can use your unique URL and link it to your affiliate website.

•   Videos - If you don't like to write, perhaps making a video would work better for you. You can tell your viewers about the benefits of your product. Then, just like the blog, you link it using your URL.

•   Articles - You can write and submit articles. When you submit the articles to directories, you include the benefits of the product/service. Always remember to link it to the affiliate with your own URL.

•   Social Media - The benefits of social media are endless. If you don't have a social media page of some kind, such as Facebook, Twitter, or LinkedIn, you need to set up at least one. You can write a blog or make a note why you're recommending this particular product/service and post your link on your wall.

• Solo Ads - You can find a list that is a good fit for your product/service with an audience that will be interested in it and buy solo ads for that product.

Chapter 4: Getting Started With Affiliate Marketing

Now you know what affiliate marketing is and how it works. If you think this may be something that will work for you, here are the basic steps you need to do to get started:

•   Choose the right niche - When you're ready to create your affiliate website, you need to decide the type of product you want to promote on the site. If you plan to place them on your blog, you'll want to think of products that are related to the subject matter of the blog. Remember, you're not stuck with this product. If it doesn't sell, you can drop it. Choosing a well-paying product that will benefit your audience is the goal.

•   Selecting the right affiliate program - You need to research and find businesses that offer you a commission-sharing program that is profitable. High commissions don't necessarily mean it's something you want to sell. The products need to be quality products that fit into your niche.

•   Planning the right strategy - The right promotional strategy is important. You need to define your target market. Knowing who your customers are and what they're interested in will make it easier for you to develop topics and discussions that will attract them and bring

traffic to your site. You'll want to be creative when you place your affiliate links. This will make your visitors be tempted to want to know more.

The more traffic you can bring to your site the better. To make a substantial amount of money, it is best to have a site that has at least 500 visitors a day. Traffic, however, is not all you need.

You can have all the traffic you could ever want, but if they don't click the merchant's link, it means nothing. You have to entice them to click that link.

Chapter 5: How to Find an Affiliate Program?

Before you can build your affiliate website, it is important that you research the affiliate programs available. Most of the programs will have a directory you can view by subject to look at all the products that are available. There are many affiliate networks available. Here are a few of them:

ClickBank.com (http://clickbank.com) - This is one of the best retail marketplaces for selling digital products like e-books or software. There you will find thousands of e-books in many different categories like: Computers/Internet, Software & Services, Arts & Entertainment, Health & Fitness, Business/Investing, Games, Cooking/Foods, Parenting, and Politics, etc. A large number of these books are written in a "how to" format. They tell you how to do something or fix a particular problem.

Since there is no manufacturing cost per item for software and eBooks, the commissions can be high. You can frequently find commissions from 50-70% on these products. There are two ways you can make money on ClickBank.

1.   Create your own products and then sell them. You have to create a vendor account so you can list your product. You determine the price of your product and how much you'll pay

an affiliate to sell it. If you have a good product, you may get many affiliates that want to sell it. You don't have to worry about all those accounts. ClickBank automatically credits the right amount into particular affiliate account. It then credits your account with the rest

2.   Work as an affiliate to promote products. You may not be able to, or have time to write dynamic eBooks. You may also not have the resources you need to manage everything. By promoting products already listed in its marketplace, you can still make money, and you don't have to do the work.

When you visit ClickBank, you'll find some statistics in their listings on affiliate programs. Here are a few of the terms you will see on the site and what they mean:

•   Initial $/sale—This is the amount you earn per sale

•   Avg %/sale—This lets you know the percentage of the sale price you will receive.

•   Avg Rebill Total—The amount you might expect in addition to the initial sale if the product has recurring billing such as monthly membership fees.

•   Avg %/Rebill - You will only see this amount if that individual vendor offers products that have recurring billing. It allows you to see the average commission rate to be earned for that amount of income.

- Grav - This lets you know how "hot" the product currently is. If the gravity is high, it means there a number of affiliates are doing well selling that product. If it shows low gravity, the number of affiliates selling this is less. Generally, you should select products which have a fairly good amount of activity by affiliates.

If you want to sign up for ClickBank, it's a pretty simple process. You just click the link that says "Sign Up." You'll find it on their home page near the top. Just insert the requested details and click "Submit." It will give you instructions to follow next. When you're signed up and have your own ClickBank ID, you'll be able to find any product you want to promote that is on the network.

Look at the products. When you find one you want to promote, simply click the link to "Promote." They'll ask for your ID. Once you give it, your HopLink, which is your affiliate link, will be created by the site. When you're browsing products you'll see a link to "Promote." Without this link, you won't get credit for your visitors that purchase the products.

Commission Junction Marketplace - This network provides extensive reach for advertisers. It also offers high rewards for publishers. It gives publishers and advertisers who join a way to access information, analyze results and manage their programs for success. Here's how it works for each:

1.   Advertisers - You can use the reporting tools on CJ Marketplace in many ways such as: Creating a call to action, defining program terms, publisher applications reviewing, and program performance analysis. They also have an online resource, CJU Online, to learn strategies, connect with publishers, and learn the latest news for the industry. .

2.   Publishers - You can apply to join programs and have access to all the inventory of links. Then you can start placing offers on your site, putting them in e-mail campaigns, or listing them in search listings.

There are also ways to find affiliate programs that operate outside affiliate networks. These won't be in the directories. Finding out about them can be a little more difficult. You can always email the merchant directly if you hear of one and ask them for details.

Sometimes you may see a program that says "Invitation Only." These sites usually restrict entry either by only admitting people who have purchased their product, or by reviewing and approving people on a case-by-case basis.

Chapter 6: Promoting Products through Affiliate Program

Review the product/service you are an affiliate of - When you begin to promote your products and services, you'll want to write a review for each one. A review is usually only one page and it contains the following information:

1. Product, service, or website name

2. Description - A brief description of the product, service or website

3. Availability - Where the item can be purchased or accessed

4. Pros - What you feel is good about the product

5. Cons - What you don't like about the product

6. Price - Do you feel the price is fair, too high, or too low

7. Recommendation - Why would you recommend this product and who would you recommend it to

8. Additional comments

9.   Contact information - Let them know the contact information of the product/service/website owner – use your affiliate link so you will get paid.

If you'd like to get products you can try out and then review on your blog, there are two ways to get them:

1.   Join a blog review network - Just complete a form with information about you and your blog. Once you do, you will get review invitations. You decide which ones you accept and which ones you decline. If you accept the invitation, you usually get a product, and it's yours to keep. You use it and then write a review. Sometimes, in addition to the product, you'll get a form of nominal compensation like a gift card or sweepstakes entry.

A few networks you may want to consider are:

•   Sponsored Reviews (http://www.sponsoredreviews.com/) -- Sponsored Reviews can be used to attract people who will write an honest product review. The incentive for them is that they'll earn cash.

•   Prizey If you become a free member, there's a chance you could get connected with a PR company.

•   MomSelect (http://www.momselect.com/) A review network that is open to both bloggers and non-bloggers.

The downside to blog networks is not being able to select the invitations you get. You may be interested in technology, and your blog may be focused on it. You want to find good products to affiliate with and you want to try them out first to see that they are quality products. However, you may get invitations for dish detergent or shampoo instead. You can decline, of course, but actually accepting and doing reviews for them gives you a good opportunity to practice writing reviews for the products you do want to become an affiliate with. They also help grow your audience, which is important. This is a great way for new bloggers to start increasing traffic to their site.

2.   Ask for them - Find the company you're interested in becoming an affiliate for. Ask them if they're interested in sending you a product you'd like to write a review on and possibly promote on your site. Tell them a little about you and your blog. It takes a little work to get your inquiry crafted so that it is clear and persuasive, but once it's done, it will be worth it.

Make sure when you accept, it's a product you think you can stand behind. In other words, if you'd never pay $100 for a pair of jeans, then don't accept the invitation when you receive it. It will be difficult for you to convince someone else to buy them. It would also be difficult for you to promote them on your site if you decided to become an affiliate.

Create a video tutorial on how the product/service works— Video tutorials are a great medium for explaining "how to" topics. You can actually show your audience how to do something, and they get a great visual which can give them a better understand of how a product/service works.

Here are the steps you should follow to prepare a good video tutorial:

1.   Write a script - Select a concept or short task you can briefly describe. You'll want to make it around 300 words, since videos are ideally three minutes and no longer than five minutes long. Make the script as much like conversation as possible. Read through it several times and actually walk through the steps you want to show your audience. Having your script on a monitor with the places where you are to perform an action highlighted can help you stay focused and on task during the video.

2.   Prepare a simulation—Determine the kind of information, event, or task you want to show and run through it. Make sure it works and you can demonstrate it in a simple way. Practice a few times so you can be sure that your actions line up with your script.

3.   Record the simulation and narration—Ideally, this is done in three steps:

- Record your script on one monitor and the simulation on another monitor. Don't worry if you find yourself slightly deviating from your script. It happens when you're trying to be conversational, and that's alright. Try to keep your voice natural, but focus on the simulation. Get clean, smooth screen action. If it's a computer simulation, don't use a touchpad mouse. The movements can be jerky. Instead, use a regular mouse and drag it smoothly. Avoid

Moving the mouse around when you talk, because it causes editing to be difficult.

- Record the audio again - You need to separate the audio from the video. Then read your script again. Make sure you pause where you need to pause. When doing this type of voiceover, try to be aware of things such as: varying the pitch of your voice, avoid rhymes that are repetitive, enunciate, speak clearly and confidently, and mix the pace of your speaking so you will sound as natural as possible.

- Match the timing - After you record the audio again, play both tracks simultaneously. Match the timing. Your pauses may not match up perfectly, but don't worry about that. You can adjust the space between audio waves and come close.

4.   Simulation post-processing - Go through the audio and the simulation and take out any long pauses that are unnecessary or any moments of inaction. You can add callouts where necessary to call attention to something you want to show on the screen. Give your video about a two-second title slide. Make sure it describes the purpose of the video. Fade in your recording as you fade out the title.

The type of software you are using will make a difference in the options you have for callouts, annotations, and animation. Just be sure to keep it as simple as possible. The more you add to your video, the greater

the file size. The greater the file size, the more time-consuming it will be to produce. If you want to integrate a music track, you can browse www.istockaudio.com to find a

5.   Publish and integrate the video – Convert the video to an MP4 format. Then upload it to your server. If you upload it to YouTube, it will automatically render it in HD. Using HD allows any text you use to show up clear and not blurry. YouTube also has voice recognition software that automatically syncs your caption with the voice. Simply upload the script in the captions section. The auto-sync program helps non-native speakers and those who have difficulty hearing to know what your video is saying. Search engine optimization is also increased.

Recommend it on your Site or Blog - Once you've created the tutorial, you want as many people to see it as possible. Remember you want quality content. If your audience is engaged and excited, then they'll come back to your site more often, and they'll stay on it longer.

It is important to remember the quality rule when you're selecting your products. A lot of bloggers don't seem to select their products by the quality. They just promote anything. Other times they may be promoting quality merchandise, but they don't seem to care how they promote it. They never use a fresh, new approach. You should take the time to consider the vendor. They care about their customers and their integrity. Poor quality promotion of their products doesn't make them look good and it certainly does not help your sales.

That's one reason video tutorials are such a hit. They give your readers a new look at an old product or a first look at a new product. It helps build trust with your audience when you provide them with content they feel is valuable.

Social media - If you're looking for a powerful medium that helps you connect with the masses, social media is it. Everyone that wants to be an affiliate marketer has to reach out to a lot of people. Social media sites can help you do precisely that. Social media can be a powerful tool for affiliate marketers. Social media websites such as Facebook, LinkedIn, and Twitter give you a chance to connect with the people from all walks of life and share what you have to say with them.

There are several things you can do through social media to help make your strategy for affiliate marketing successful. They include:

• Promotion of the affiliate programs - Once you've developed your own following, those listed in your friend's list will be able to see and repost all of your posts and links. You can promote the products for which you are an affiliate through posts and blogs on your page. Fan pages can be created as well, which will help to improve the promotion for you.

• Bond with your audience - You can increase the number of your contacts by adding people that will appreciate what you have to say. By creating interactive groups, you will have better coordination with your audience. Once you share the information about your affiliate products with the audience, ask them for their feedback. Feedback can be valuable in both building bonds with your audience and to make needed modifications to your strategy. Let them know about your affiliate products and ask for feedback.

• Stay up-to-date - You'll want to keep current on what is happening in your market area. Through social media, you can learn about all of the new product launches, and which ones the public really seems to like. This will help you to know the current trends and help you fine tune your affiliate marketing strategies in the right direction.

Since you won't be the only affiliate marketer the competition is high to make your strategy successful. Here are a few tips that will help you get an edge over the market on social media sites:

• Focus on relationships - Sites such as Facebook, Google+ and Twitter are social media sites. The key word there is "social." Make sure you make connections with the right people and build a good rapport with them. Try having a fan page that is numberless. This will help you gain more information. Building a good, strong relationship with your prospective clients will help with promotion. They'll want to pass on what you have to say with friends on their page.

• Add social bookmarking - You can put a social bookmarking button on your website. Then, ask your visitors to follow. This way, if people who visit your posts like them, is easy for them to share. There is no charge for using social bookmarking, so take advantage of it.

- Blog smarter...not harder - Some bloggers work very hard and spend hour after hour preparing blogs that are seldom seen. When creating blog posts you plan to post on your site, blog smart. The main focus should be to grab the attention of the visitor. Once you do, give them informative, precise information that they will find valuable. If you do this, your social media presence will increase.

Boosting your web presence is important, and these tips will help you do it. Once you have a firm grasp of social media, you'll find it easier to find and connect with potential clients. Once you've chosen the right products/services to promote, just be honest with your prospective customers. If you do, you can win their hearts through social media.

Email list - A lot of bloggers don't feel they can make money with email marketing, so they don't use it. They fail to see the advantages. They just feel that it's not worth their time, so they don't try it. Just like a new restaurant...you won't know what it's like if you don't try it. You may be missing out on something great.

There are some factors you don't want to overlook as a blogger that will later be realized as a mistake. Here are a few things you need to be aware of before you begin your email marketing campaign:

• Build your subscriber's list - You want to have as many as subscribers as possible on your list. If your email were a blog, you'd have traffic to it. In email marketing, your subscribers are your traffic. The more traffic you have for your blog, the better the results. It's the same with email and subscribers. The more you have, the greater the results.

• Be original - Many people using email marketing fail to be original in their emails. This is one of the best ways to turn subscribers into un-subscribers. If people don't feel your emails contain original, valuable information, they'll unsubscribe in a heartbeat. They don't want their inbox cluttered with garbage.

• Write to prove you're familiar with what you're promoting - Nothing is worse than a "canned" review taken straight from ad copy. Readers want to feel that you know what you're talking about. They're looking for a personal touch that shows you know the product. If you can, request the product and use it first. This gives you first-hand knowledge to share with your reader. This way, you'll be better able to answer questions your readers might have about the products.

• Write honest reviews - Every product you review won't be "awesome." Some will just be "average." Whatever the case may be, just say so. You can give your reviews a simple number rating like 1—2—3—4—5. Be sure, however, to give it the rating you feel it deserves.

•   Don't use too many links - Links are great, and you do want to use them, but there's no use to have five links in the first paragraph on the same keyword. You can limit the number of your links if you are more creative and effective with the ones you use. For example: Have graphical banners that are custom made which say things like, "Learn more about the product," "View the product," or "Checkout my review." These let the reader know exactly what they'll be getting at the other end of the link. These attract the reader, and peak their interest in the product.

Chapter 7: How to Promoting Products through Affiliate program

If it was a piece of cake to build a profitable website, everyone would be doing it. Building a website in itself isn't that difficult. Building one that can help you make a good amount of affiliate case, however, can be a bit more difficult. If you want to build a site that makes you a successful affiliate marketer here are a few steps you should follow when you create your site:

• Give your customers what they want on your site - People will tell you there's no "magic formula" for success in building an affiliate website. While this may be true to some extent, there are a few things your customer will want that will help make your site successful. These include:

1. Quality content - I can't stress enough how important it is to give your readers content that they will value and appreciate. Filler content just won't cut it. When you create your site, focus on building one that gives your readers revolutionary new information, quality advice, and valuable resources.

Remember that it's just as easy for a reader to "click out" of your site as it is for them to "click on" it. I'm sure you've searched for something on Google and found a site that looked interesting by the title. You open it, and find something that doesn't give you any help whatsoever. The first thing you do then is click the "back" button and go back to the search to look for something that does give you something you can use.

Your readers will do the same thing. Give your readers information you would find valuable. Everything on your website—your articles, your blog posts, your videos, your pictures, etc—should give the reader what they were searching for. This will, more than likely, make them want to continue reading. It may also make them want to make a purchase.

If you're worried about providing quality content, here are a few tips that will guide you:

Don't try to optimize your site solely for search engines. Optimize them for the people who visit your site and will read it. If you do this, you'll get more people to your site, so the search engine numbers will take care of themselves.

• Research your content thoroughly to be sure it is correct. Just like giving quality content adds a positive impact to your site, giving your readers incorrect information can have a negative impact on your site.

• Give the reader what you say you're going to give them. There's nothing worse than wasting your time reading an article that doesn't tell you what it says it's going to. If you say you're going to give them 10 ways to overcome their fears, you should give them 10 ways to overcome their fears. If your title suggests it, and they click on you in the search, make them glad you did by giving them the valuable information they want.

2. A design that is neat, attractive easy to use design - Thank goodness the days of ugly websites are coming to an end. It isn't acceptable to have tacky animated graphics or banner ads on your site. Often, however, you still see affiliate marketing sites that look like they came from the '90's.

Your website is your potential customer's first look at you. It gives them an overall impression of you. You want it to be one that will inspire confidence so people will trust you. Visit other sites online. Look at the ones that make you want to read them and the ones that make you want to click out immediately. If you don't have a site that is neat, attractive, and easy to use, it will look unprofessional and make your viewers hit the dreaded "back" button.

You don't have to have difficult coding know how or purchase expensive design software to have a really nice, professional looking website. On programs like WordPress, you can create a great site with a few clicks of the mouse and an attractive theme. That means there's no reason at all you should have an old-looking, unattractive site.

3. Great opt-in forms - Although there may be some exceptions to the saying that "the money is in the list," it is basically a solid framework for getting the most for your money in affiliate marketing. You can build good relationships with your readers by encouraging them to "opt in" to your list. As a result, you may also be able to increase your profits through the use of pre-selling and by having multiple sales per customer.

Getting people to do this isn't as easy as it may seem. One of the biggest challenges you may face as an affiliate who uses email marketing is implementing opt in forms and squeeze pages that are able to convert your readers to members of your list. You can have great content and pre-sells, but if your opt-in forms are ugly or misplaced, you may end up with only a few subscribers.

You can create effective opt-in forms that give you an unstoppable opt-in magnet if you have two important things:

• A great hook - The hook should be something that makes people want to subscribe to your list when they see it. It might be an eBook that they would usually have to pay $30 dollars for that you're giving them for free. It may be a free gift of some kind. Whatever it is, write the hook so that it sounds irresistible! Make them think, "Wow, they're giving that to me for free just for signing up? I'd be stupid to turn that down."

• Opt-in forms that convert - You should design them with high conversions in mind. Make sure they're attractive. You want to make sure they are well placed. Place them where they will be clearly seen but not in a manner that they distract from your content.

4. First-rate customer service - If you have a competitor that offers pretty much the same merchandise, one way to win customers over that competitor is to have better customer service. I mean if site one and site two are alike, and site one has bad customer service, where is the customer going to go...straight to site 2— YOU!

You can have the most attractive website in the world with the most attractive, well-placed opt-ins, but it won't matter a bit if you don't treat your customers with the respect and courtesy they deserve.

You don't have to handle their orders or returns, but you still need to offer customer service. You need to make sure that you reply to email inquiries, blog comments, and even complaints promptly. Be kind and courteous in your replies and try to give your customers the answers they want. If you don't know, don't say, "I don't know." Look it up! Sure, they could look it up themselves, but then you might lose them as a customer. If you take the time to look it up for them, they'll remember that. They'll also pass on to their friends how kind you were to them. This will give you that "site 2" customer service that wins over that "site one" site in the battle for new and returning customers.

If you want to build an affiliate website that will bring you good profits, you need to make sure you do it right. Make sure it has everything you need and make sure it's done in the right manner. A good baker wouldn't leave out ingredients or add salt instead of sugar. Put in everything you need to and do it right and you'll have a successful, professional looking website.

CHAPTER 8 - CONCLUSION

If done correctly, affiliate marketing can be a profitable business. The thing to remember, however, is that it does require some work on your part. You can't just set up a site and do nothing. You have to promote your items. The more you do and the more effectively you do it, the more you'll sell.

Affiliate marketing isn't something you can dive into with enthusiasm and give up after a few weeks with no profit. Building your audience, email lists, and customers takes a little time. Patience is a virtue—stick with it, and your patience will be rewarded. Be impatient and give up, and you'll fail.

In order to succeed in affiliate marketing, you really need to get passionately involved. You need to actively work to grow your business and to solving your reader's problems.

It is important to remember that doing things just for the money seldom works out right. That's why you should select products you would use yourself. Be passionate about them and have confidence in them, and you'll be able to promote them more effectively. It's easier to write about things you are confident in. Sometimes, that won't even seem like work to you because you enjoy doing it.

Affiliate marketing isn't for everyone, but if you've bought this book, and read this far, you're definitely interested in it. One key thing you need to remember is that "without customers, you have no business." That's a very literal comment, but it's also a very powerful comment with two separate and definite meanings:

1. If you don't promote your product and attract potential customers to your site, then it's pretty much useless to have a site. You'll never make a profit if the customers never see your products. Know your target market and find ways to get them to see what you have to offer. Promote it in a way that will attract them to your site.

2. Your customers are your lifeline—treat them well! Don't give up once you've attracted customers. Know you need them to keep your business profitable. Focus your business on those customers. Get to know your customers and what they're looking for. You can survey your target

market to find out exactly what they want. Once you know that, give it to them.

One of the biggest mistakes an affiliate marketer can make is to misjudge their customers. It's not enough to think you can sell product X because someone else did and made a profit. If your audience is only interested in product Y, then you'll never sell product X to them. What you should be offering instead is product Y. Your customer's wants and needs should be what your site is all about. Tell them what they want to know and offer products they want to buy, and you'll have satisfied customers and your audience will grow.

People who are passionate about the niche they work in and truly like the products they sell can do really well in affiliate marketing. This is because they believe in what they're selling and enjoy what they're doing. That doesn't mean you have to be passionate about it to make a profit, you don't. What you do need to be, however, is dedicated to it. It's YOUR business. YOU decide what to sell. YOU decide how you want to promote it, and YOU have to do the work. It does take a little effort, but by doing the right research, finding the right products, and promoting them in the right way, YOU will be the one making the profit!

ABOUT THE AUTHOR

IQ Press, Inc. is a small publishing company dedicated to providing access to educational materials primarily in small business start-up and development. Their mission is to bring the reader useful information that can be implemented with a small capital outlay and generate income streams for the reader to implement.

We hope you enjoy these reports and that they will help improve your life.

To get a jumpstart in online marketing download our exclusive quick start guide here: www.IQPress.org/Quickstart

Check out more great reports at:

www.IQPress.org

REFERENCE MATERIALS

Other books you may enjoy to help you on your journey:

Affiliate Marketing for Beginners. Have you heard about affiliate marketing but not quite sure if it's real or really works? This definitive guide will lay out the ins and outs of this interesting field. Filled with tips and hints, it also has information on what to look out for.

Affiliate marketing truly can be started with very little money and has the potential for great rewards. Simple to start with the right guidance, affiliate marketing seriously reduces the risk in starting your own business. Imagine a business with little investment, no inventory, no customer service, no shipping and handling and no risk! Further it can grow to replace your current income and still be operated as a part-time operation. All you need is the enclosed information and you're ready to start.

Finding the Best Affiliate Products to Promote: How do I find the best products to sell? Now that you know about affiliate marketing and its great income potential, how can you choose what product(s) to promote? You want one with high demand but not too much competition. You need to choose the category, the product, the venue, the program, etc... That's quite a lot for a new company owner! We can help. This guide will walk you through all these decisions and keep you from getting in a bad place with a product that has poor sell-through.

Affiliate Marketing and Success Systems: This report is a compendium of tips and ideas to help keep you on track with your affiliate marketing business. You want an automatic money machine? We'll show you not only how to grow but also to get that growth on autopilot! With a few simple programs you can get the company to generate a continuous income stream. That's why you went into this type business, right?

Using this report will turbocharge your results and help you simply and effectively grow your sales. Bring in a constant stream of new customers and new products to offer your existing customers for a generous income. You could even quit your job if you wanted! Imagine all that free time while still enjoying a great income.

Available exclusively at: www.IQPress.org

www.ingramcontent.com/pod-product-compliance
Lightning Source LLC
La Vergne TN
LVHW052316060326
832902LV00021B/3915